- Bankruptcy -

10 Big Mistakes You Want to Avoid

(Everything You Wanted to Know But Were Afraid to Ask)

By David Walden & Donald DiCarlo
http://www.bankruptcy101.us/

Table of Contents

Introduction

"10 Big Mistakes You Want to Avoid" is a Quick Reference Guide to Bankruptcy that is concise and covers the ten key areas you will want to avoid when filing your Bankruptcy.

The information presented here is the result of hundreds of bankruptcy filings over a period of 12 plus years and includes methods used for keeping every one of my clients out of trouble. The philosophy has been a conservative one; avoid any practice that has even the slightest chance of raising one red flag with the Bankruptcy Court.

The benefit of using such a conservative approach is in part what this book is about.

Applying the tools found here will help you to go through the entire bankruptcy filing process without one red flag.

The approach I used with my clients is no different than what I would do if I were preparing to file my own bankruptcy.

One thing I don't want in the bankruptcy filing process is even one red flag!

The other thing I don't want is the Bankruptcy Court or my Bankruptcy Attorney deciding for me which chapter of bankruptcy I would file under!

Why is that such a bad idea?

The Bankruptcy Court and your Bankruptcy Attorney will determine the chapter for your bankruptcy filing based upon guidelines designed by and to serve the best interests of Your Creditors and <u>Not You</u>!

Likewise the guidelines for Chapter 13 Bankruptcy are designed to pay as much back to the unsecured creditors as is possible no matter what the cost to you and your family!

By following the procedures outlined in Ultimate Bankruptcy 2010 you will avoid most if not all of the pitfalls and mistakes associated with filing either Chapter 7 or Chapter 13 Bankruptcy.

You will take complete control over every aspect of your bankruptcy filing process including which chapter you ultimately end up filing under.

Filing the bankruptcy chapter that is best for you can save you tens of thousands of dollars and years of misery and more.

Pre-planning your bankruptcy is crucial for assuring maximum benefit to your situation no matter what chapter you end up filing under.

The millions of dollars spent on bankruptcy reform by the banking and credit industry will not destroy your right to debt relief through bankruptcy no matter what has been planned by the corporate bankers.

The Banking Industry may have changed the bankruptcy rules in 2005 but "Ultimate Bankruptcy 2010" changes the game plan.

In the end, you will end up filing under the chapter that best serves your needs and gives you minimum loss with maximum benefit!

The second part of this book covers 10 essential areas you will want to consider when designing your bankruptcy game plan.

These areas include; when and how you file your bankruptcy as well as key information you will need to provide to the bankruptcy court as a part of the filing process.

This key information is what the bankruptcy court will use to evaluate the legitimacy of your bankruptcy petition. Areas such as property transfers, financial transactions, unreported income and contradictory red flag areas.

It is crucial that you play by the rules and win through effective strategy rather than attempting anything that looks even remotely suspicious!

In this respect the ideal Bankruptcy Attorney is like the ideal Game Coach in that they will call all of the right plays for a home run at every turn.

For this reason it is crucial that you follow the directions in "Ultimate Bankruptcy 2010" for finding the best Bankruptcy Attorney in your area and retain that attorney.

Once you locate and retain the best Bankruptcy Attorney for your team you will then have the ultimate winning combination for the most effective Bankruptcy experience possible.

Be sure to check out our website for more bankruptcy information and new products as they are released:

http://www.bankruptcy101.us/

10 Big Mistakes You Want To Avoid

Mistake #1: <u>Not</u> Pre-Planning You Bankruptcy at Least (6) Months prior to actually filing.

Pre-planning your bankruptcy is most essential in today's tough bankruptcy climate.

What does this mean exactly?

You need to approach your bankruptcy not as a personal failure but as a business enterprise where you can win or lose big time depending on the actions you take today.

You need to clearly understand the difference between filing Chapter 7 and Chapter 13 Bankruptcy and decide which one will best serve your needs?

Chapter 13 Bankruptcy: The major question you need to ask when considering Chapter 13 Bankruptcy is: Do you have property you need to protect or non-dischargeable debts that you will need from 3 – 5 years to pay off in a Chapter 13 Plan Payment?

If your answer is no then what are you doing filing a Chapter 13 Bankruptcy?

If you have equity in your home and wish to protect it from foreclosure Chapter 13 is for you.

If you have debts that cannot be discharged through Chapter 7 Bankruptcy like IRS Debt or Child Support Payments and you need to reduce the strain on your budget then Chapter 13 may be right for you.

If filing for Bankruptcy under Chapter 13 offers you no real advantage then you really need to take the steps necessary to avoid it and clarify this with your Bankruptcy Attorney.

If Chapter 13 Bankruptcy is not right for you then you need to take actions to adjust your budget in such a way that it will allow you to file for Chapter 7 Bankruptcy.

You can discuss the options with your Bankruptcy Attorney or when you are making your FREE Bankruptcy Consultation rounds.

You need to do your pre-planning at least SIX MONTHS in advance so that you can get things out of the way well outside of the period that the Bankruptcy Court will be focusing on when evaluating your Bankruptcy Information.

Talk with your Bankruptcy Attorney about any questions you may have on this subject.

Mistake #2: Having your Bankruptcy Attorney or the Bankruptcy Court tell you what Chapter to file under.

One of the most crucial aspects of Filing Your Bankruptcy is what Chapter of Bankruptcy you will eventually end up filing under.

If left in the hands of your Bankruptcy Attorney or the Bankruptcy Court you will end up filing according to a pre-designed set of parameters that service the desires of the Banking and Credit Card Industries.

You need to decide what chapter you will file under once you take an objective look at your situation and see if filing Chapter 13 Bankruptcy serves any real purpose for you.

Everything you do from this moment forward related to your Bankruptcy filing must fall in line with this decision.

Chapter 13 Bankruptcy: If you decide that Chapter 13 might be best for you because of your individual circumstance then you need to work with your Bankruptcy Attorney to maximize your benefits under that chapter.

You need to begin designing your life and ultimately your income to debt ratio so that it fits your ultimate Bankruptcy Objective.

If Chapter 13 is best for your situation you need to determine that magic number, the actual amount of your desired plan payment, so that it covers all of the debt that you need to pay off plus about an additional 2% to cover the unsecured creditors.

That would be an ideal scenario so that you only pay the debt that you need to in this process.

That means that the money left over on the positive side after covering all of your cost of living expense is equal to the amount needed to pay the secured and priority debt and little else.

If you are re-affirming your real estate loan because you are keeping your home then you need to include your monthly mortgage amount in your cost of living Bankruptcy Schedule J.

Remember you must keep all monthly payments current for your mortgage while your arrears are paid off in the Chapter 13 Bankruptcy Plan.

You need to create your initial budget and present this to your Bankruptcy Attorney then work with them from this point forward.

Chapter 7 Bankruptcy: If you have determined that this is your best way to go then you need to design your life and your budget to reflect that you have no money left after paying your cost of living and secured monthly bills each month.

If your plan is to file Chapter7 you will need to begin making the necessary changes required in order to support your plan and make this work effectively (see "Ultimate Bankruptcy 2010" for more information).

Mistake #3: <u>Not</u> Treating your Bankruptcy Case as though it were an extremely important Business Transaction.

It is a Big Mistake to treat your Bankruptcy Case as though it is anything less than a major business transaction involving significant dollar and property losses and gains.

As mentioned above, your approach to your Bankruptcy can either be one of sorrow and remorse or one that is conducted with an attitude of a business person conducting a business transaction that can involve a great deal of money and resources.

Attitude is king in the world of Bankruptcy as it is in most areas of our lives.

In the Bankruptcy experience Attitude can make the difference between indentured servitude status and real financial freedom.

Mistake #4: <u>Not</u> Pre-Screening the Bankruptcy Attorneys in your area.

You need to determine which of your local Bankruptcy Attorneys is the most knowledgeable, available, reliable, and most ethical, and the one who will truly be on your side.

One of the key elements of a truly successful Bankruptcy is having a Bankruptcy Attorney who is on your side ... highly ethical ... reliable ... and answers the messages and phone calls you make.

As described before it is crucial that you interview at least (3) Bankruptcy Attorneys in your area to learn all that you can about the Bankruptcy Filing Process.

It is just as crucial that you are screening every one of these Bankruptcy Attorneys you are meeting with to be certain that you retain the very best one for your Bankruptcy.

Mistake #5: <u>Not</u> using a solid reference source like "Ultimate Bankruptcy 2010" to effectively plan your Bankruptcy.

If you do not use an alternative Information source like "Ultimate Bankruptcy 2010" then you will be left at the mercy of rules set in motion by the Banking and Credit Card Lobbyists back in 2005 and this is one huge mistake!

It is imperative that you do not fall further victim to this group of scoundrels any more than each of us already has through their deceptive and fraudulent banking practices!

Everything covered in "Ultimate Bankruptcy 2010" has been designed to protect and to allow the reader to get every possible advantage with the existing system when filing their Bankruptcy.

The "Bankruptcy Control System", "Bankruptcy Checklist", "Critical Questions List, and Bankruptcy Work List are tools that have been designed and provided here to assist you in every way possible.

Mistake #6: <u>Not</u> designing your budget yourself but relying on your Bankruptcy Attorney or the Bankruptcy Court.

You Budget is perhaps the most crucial part of your Bankruptcy as well as your key element for your Pre-Planning Process.

Your budget along with your Schedules I & J and the "Means Test" will determine not only what Chapter of Bankruptcy you will be permitted to file under but also what your life might look like over the next 3 to 5 years.

You do need to decide for yourself precisely what you are wanting before you even begin this process.

For instance, you need to know the rules of engagement and how you will get what you want before you even begin.

If you see that your budget has too much left over income at the end of each month and you know that filing chapter 7 Bankruptcy is best for you then you will need to figure out how you will decrease your income or increase your monthly expenses in a way that the Bankruptcy Court will approve!

Here is the catch!

You may need to change your source of income to make this happen if adjusting your expenses will not work for you. What we are talking about can mean that you may need to look for another job that pays you less for the short term.

You or your spouse may have to give up their job or take reduced hours in order for you to qualify for Chapter 7.

You or your spouse may need to take more hours or additional work in order to qualify for filing a Chapter 13 Bankruptcy.

You need to look at how much you will end up paying out in a (5) Year Chapter 13 Bankruptcy Plan especially if filing under Chapter 13 serves no real purpose for your particular situation?

You need to do the math!

Since most Chapter 13 Bankruptcies are for (5) years these days and if after you deduct your living expenses from your income you still have $350 per month left then here is what your plan might look like:

Monthly Payment of $350.00 X 60 Months = $21,000.00!

If that surplus amount is higher the chart below might apply.

Monthly Payment of $550.00 X 60 Months = $33,000.00!

Monthly Payment of $850.00 X 60 Months = $51,000.00!

And so on down the line ...

You will need to ask yourself a few questions related to this scenario:

How long would it take me to save up $33,000.00 in the current economy and state of affairs?

What will my quality of life be like during the entire Plan Payment experience?

How will filing a Chapter 13 Bankruptcy affect my ability to get my Credit back?

Is it better for me to give up some income now for say (3) or (4) months in order to avoid giving up all of that money and to end up living like an indentured servant during the entire (5) year period?

See what other questions you can come up related to this scenario.

Discuss any concerns you might have with your Bankruptcy Attorney.

Mistake #7: <u>Not</u> using a proven Check List Tool like the one included in "Ultimate Bankruptcy 2010".

If you are not using a proven Check List Tool to manage and direct your Bankruptcy Filing Process it is far easier to slip and miss key issues that can cost you big time!

I don't need to go into a discussion here about the value of using a Checklist when working in critical areas that can heavily affect the quality of your life for you and your family.

Just check out this the Boeing Website at the link below for info on how important use of a Checklist is with any critical operation:

http://www.boeing.com/news/frontiers/archive/20 06/april/i_ca3.html

If using a Checklist works for huge operation like Boeing then it will definitely work for you as well!

Make certain that you have gone through and PRINTED the "Bankruptcy Checklist" included in both

"Ultimate Bankruptcy 2010" or "Bankruptcy Boot Camp 2010".

If you can think of any other items specific to your case then be certain to add them to this list in the order that they will need to be completed.

Be certain to review and PRINT out the other tools also provided in this book.

Mistake #8: <u>**Not**</u> **completing Schedules (I) & (J) and "Means Test" six months prior to filing to help you determine what chapter you will file under.**

If you are even thinking about filing for Bankruptcy then early completion of Schedules I & J and the "Means Test" is almost imperative!

Only after you have had at least two of your FREE Bankruptcy Consultations and have done your initial Schedules I & J and the "Means Test" **Can you even begin to consider what Chapter of Bankruptcy is best for you to file under!** The type in the last sentence is in Bolt Type for a good reason!

Only after experiencing your FREE Bankruptcy Consultations will you have a much better understanding of how the Bankruptcy Process works.

You will know more about the Bankruptcy Process and which Chapter will benefit your situation the most.

You will have most or all of your questions answered and learn all that you need to by working your plan and being prepared for each of your Bankruptcy Consultations.

It is important that you are prepared for your Bankruptcy Consultations by having all of your bankruptcy questions completed in advance.

By planning and being prepared you will learn everything you need to do in order to improve the quality of life for you and your family for years to come.

You will be left with little doubt regarding what Chapter of Bankruptcy you will want to file under.

Only then will you know if you have the kind of debt and assets that would most warrant your filing a Chapter 13 or Chapter 7 Bankruptcy.

You can then make the needed adjustments from there so that you qualify for the Chapter you have targeted.

Mistake #9: <u>Not</u> setting aside enough cash to handle all of your bankruptcy expenses.

One thing that you need to pay close attention to is the fact that once you begin the bankruptcy filing process you will no longer be able to use your credit cards!

You will need to pay for Bankruptcy Attorney Fees, Bankruptcy Filing Fees and of course you will need money to cover your personal survival expenses during the actual bankruptcy filing period.

If you are used to living with the convenience that Credit Cards can provide you will need to revise your way of living.

Once you begin the bankruptcy filing process you will be living in a Cash Economy.

Whether you are unemployed or under employed It is always best to play it safe when you are in a financial crunch.

First of all it is important to set aside enough money, well in advance, to cover all of your Bankruptcy Filing Expenses including Bankruptcy Attorney Fees and Bankruptcy Filing Fees.

If you are planning on filing a Chapter 7 Bankruptcy then it would be a good Idea to have cash funds or travelers checks or money orders set aside for emergency use.

The same is true even if you are filing for Chapter 13 Bankruptcy where your cash or "play money" is determined or set when you design your Schedule J (Expenditure Statement).

It really does not matter which Chapter of Bankruptcy you are filing under, the reality is that in most cases you will no longer have any CREDIT CARDS or CREDIT ACCOUNTS of any kind!

Essentially, all purchases from this point forward become CASH Purchases.

This also includes things like visits to the Dentist, co-pay amounts on medical plans, medication purchases and so on down the line.

The same goes for unexpected expenses like auto repairs, auto maintenance costs and other unexpected charges that you may have normally paid with one of your credit card accounts!

The period SIX MONTHS PRIOR TO ACTUALLY FILING is kind of your pre-planning stage of your Bankruptcy Filing Experience and all important preparation is best completed in this time period.

Remember, even when you are filing for Chapter 7 Bankruptcy you are expected by the Bankruptcy Court to have some form of income.

One main issue that can exist is if your income is too high when compared with your cost of living expenses.

When there is "too much income" and not enough allotted expense then you are looking at having to file Chapter 13 ... Period!

If that is the case you will then need to take actions discussed elsewhere in this book and in "Ultimate Bankruptcy 2010".

The point here is that you have set aside an emergency fund just in case you have a situation arise where you need to have back-up funds available that you can rely on.

This applies whether you are filing Chapter 7 or Chapter 13 Bankruptcy.

Mistake #10: Over-Manipulating budget figures to help you qualify for a Better Bankruptcy Deal.

If you are inflating your living expenses in order to allow you to qualify for a Chapter 7 Bankruptcy then you are asking for trouble.

By the same token if you are inflating your living expenses to try to keep your Chapter 13 Plan Payment amount minimized then you are equally asking for trouble.

Designing your Budget and particularly Schedules I & J might be one of the most crucial elements of your Bankruptcy Planning Experience.

It is critical to know just how far you are able to go with your Cost of living expenses without offending the Bankruptcy Court. This can be tricky business in a setting like today where the level of scrutiny can be extreme!

To deal with this issue you need to be specific with your claims and be ready to document them with valid proof.

For instance if you have medical expenses that you are claiming in the amount of $650.00 per month then you had better itemize each expense and be able to prove it with valid receipts!

If you merely say Monthly Medical Expenses: $650.00 you can expect trouble and that is something you definitely Do Not Want in the Bankruptcy Court.

If your cost is this high then you need to itemize each expense:

Co-Pay on Medications........... $250.00
Co-Pay on Doctor visits $150.00
Medications not covered ....$ 75.00

And so on down the line.

If you make inflated claims on your expenses in order to avoid a Chapter 7 Bankruptcy then you had better know for certain that the Bankruptcy Court will accept what you are claiming.

This is where having a really client oriented and well informed Bankruptcy Attorney is crucial.

Make certain that you have a Bankruptcy Attorney that will take your telephone calls and give you adequate time and assistance.

Your Bankruptcy Attorney will know through experience in the Bankruptcy court just what the Bankruptcy Trustee will accept as valid and what they will hassle you over on your budget.

Once you know what is acceptable to the Bankruptcy Court you will then be able to do whatever is necessary to either lower you income figures or to create added expenses that will not serve to sabotage your filing under the chapter of bankruptcy you desire.

I have known clients who have gone out and financed a new car purchase in order to increase their monthly expenses in a way that was acceptable to the Bankruptcy Court.

Purchasing a new car allowed them to do more than just increase their total cost of living.

First off the addition of the monthly payment for their new car served to increase their expenses to the degree that they easily qualified for a Chapter 7 Bankruptcy or significantly lowered their Chapter 13 Plan Payment Amount.

Secondly the new car purchase provided reliable transportation that was covered by a 100,000 mile warranty and assured that the working member of the family would always get to work on time without hassles created by having to rely on an unreliable automobile.

Also, because of the new car warranty the family budget would not be sacrificed due to expensive automotive repair bills.

10 Essentials You Will Want To Consider

Essential #1: Listing of all major property transfers made Less Than (6) Months Prior to filing bankruptcy.

One thing you want to do in order to keep your Bankruptcy Petition from being brought into question is to disclose each and every property transfer that you have been involved with especially less than six months prior to filing.

These transfers would involve any property valued at $500 or more and would include autos, boats, motorcycles, RV equipment of any kind, etc.

This is why your Pre-Planning stages of your Bankruptcy Filing are so crucial.

You need to take care of all matters involving finances or property transfers at least six months out where your behavior will not appear as suspicious on any level.

For all property transfers made to anyone where there is certification or contract or required government title transfer or documentation of any kind (as required with an automobile title transfer for instance) then you need to list each one.

For property transfers to family members where there is no receipt or paper trail then you may be able to exclude them.

As with all cases where there are any questions or uncertainty then talk with your Bankruptcy Attorney regarding property transfers and get their recommendations on this subject.

Essential #2: Listing of Any checks cashed in the amount of $500 or more (6) months or less prior to filing your bankruptcy.

This is another area where your caution needs to be exercised.

The key thing to consider here is that in order to cash any check or financial instrument there is an immediate paper trail with the institution who cashes the check and a record that can be located somewhere.

It is important to consider what the trade off will be here. You need to ask yourself what would be the benefit of trying to hide something that is not going to affect your Bankruptcy Filing any way.

It is important to discuss any considerations with your Bankruptcy Attorney before taking action to make sure you are not just spinning your wheels for nothing.

Essential #3: Listing all Major Purchases ($1,000 or more even if made more than (6) Months Prior to filing bankruptcy.

Another key area of careful scrutiny involves the disclosure of any and all major purchases made even if made more than (6) prior to filing bankruptcy.

All documented purchases (those with receipts or registration of any kind) including those made with cash funds are transactions you may want to disclose in your Bankruptcy paperwork.

You do not want the Bankruptcy Court finding assets that you have not disclosed … period!

Even if your purchase was made with cash if the purchase is documented anywhere you may want to be sure to disclose it.

This kind of documented purchase would include things like boats, cars, RV's, jet ski's and anything where a transfer of title is involved.

Don't mean to sound like a broken record here but check with your Bankruptcy Attorney regarding all such transactions.

Remember you are paying for legal services so do not be afraid to use you attorney for advice since that is what you are paying for in part.

Essential #4: Not Making Any Cash Advances of any kind on Credit Cards during last (6) before filing.

It is critically important that you do not have any cash advances totaling $500 or more during the last (6) Months prior to actually filing your bankruptcy.

it is best not to take significantly large or repeated cash advances even six months or less prior to filing.

CAUTION: Do not take any cash advances within the six month period prior to filing bankruptcy!

Remember every transaction you make on your credit card(s) is documented and available.

It is imperative that you do not take any cash advances from your credit cards during the last six month prior to your actually filing your bankruptcy.

Do not take any cash advances in large amounts even before the six month period.

Never take any cash advances after you have told any one of your creditors that you may have to or are considering filing for Bankruptcy!

Always consult your Bankruptcy Attorney regarding any such transactions made.

Essential #5: Listing of all Major Assets or Properties of any significant value.

You will need to list all major assets ($1000 or more) no matter when acquired. (Discuss with your attorney to be certain)

Once again it is critically important to deal with this topic with caution.

It is extremely important that you do not attempt to hide anything especially when the information is readily available.

Read the recommendations in the previous topic area to get a good understanding on this subject.

Discuss all such transaction with your attorney.

Essential #6: Being Completely Truthful about All Family Sources of Income.

You will need to be completely truthful when disclosing all sources and amounts of family income being claimed:

One thing you do not want to do in the Bankruptcy Filing Process is to lie and especially about your income!

You need to be careful about not disclosing even "under the table" income.

Why?

Well, what if for any reason the person you are working for under the table becomes angered with you even after the discharge of your bankruptcy and decides to report you to the Bankruptcy Court?

If you think that this does not happen I ask you to think again!

Or what if a friend of yours becomes angry with you or a business associate or person from work who knows about this extra income wants to wreak havoc on your life.

Think carefully about what you are doing at all times and what the consequences may look like.

Essential #7: Lease/Purchase of a New Vehicle that will be reliable for you and family.

Lease or purchase a new vehicle if this is something that you need for your job or family transportation.

This is extremely important if you feel your current vehicle is going to cost you significant repair bills or is not reliable. (see "Ultimate Bankruptcy 2010" for more info on this topic)

One good possibility for dealing with "too much" income when working on your Bankruptcy Schedules is the purchase or lease of a new vehicle.

If you need added expenses in order to qualify for a Chapter 7 Bankruptcy or to lower you plan payment in a Chapter 13 Bankruptcy it may be relevant for you to consider purchasing or leasing a new car.

When such a purchase is made six months or more prior to filing your Chapter 7 Bankruptcy there should be no problems at all. Discuss this with your Bankruptcy Attorney.

When such a purchase is made even one month prior to filing a Chapter 13 Bankruptcy I have never known of even one problem arising. Discuss this with your Bankruptcy Attorney.

Essential #8: Listing of all creditors you owe money to.

You may not want to list your cousin who loaned you $400 but it is important that you list all people you owe money to including Friends, Family Members and favored creditors like doctors and dentists and business associates.

Even though you may not want to list certain creditors on your Bankruptcy Petition, because you like them or because they are family or because they are favored creditors, it is important for you to list each one and every one of them.

By listing all of your creditors you will be following the directive of the Bankruptcy Court.

Even though you have a person listed on your Bankruptcy Petition as a creditor this does not mean that you will not pay them later on when you can afford to.

Listing a person as a creditor on you bankruptcy simply means that you owe money to them… Period.

If you have a creditor whose services are extremely important to you then you do not have to let them know you are filing for Bankruptcy as long as you pay them off prior to filing.

You do not have to list anyone as long as you pay your balance with them down to -0- 6 months prior to filing your petition.

And finally by listing all creditors it does offer you maximum protection and takes the matter out of your hands because you are required to list all people you owe money to by the bankruptcy court.

Essential #9: Scheduling of at least (3) FREE Bankruptcy Consultations in your area.

Prior to actually beginning the Pre-Planning of your Bankruptcy you will need to schedule at least (3) FREE Consultations.

These Consultations will not only provide you with the information you need but will also be a great opportunity for you to interview the Bankruptcy Attorneys to see which one is right for you. (Please refer to "Ultimate Bankruptcy 2010" for detailed info)

This is one of the most important activities you will conduct during your bankruptcy pre-planning and filing experience!

It is during your (3) FREE Bankruptcy Consultations that you will gain all of the information you need to know for your bankruptcy filing and then some.

Consider this as your educational element where you will learn how this entire process works and how to deal with it effectively.

As a part of this process you will learn which Bankruptcy Attorney seems to be the best informed, most available, most reliable and the one who returns their telephone calls and will be there for you when you need them.

You will also learn which Bankruptcy Attorney will be on your team and supportive of getting you the most out of your Bankruptcy filing experience.

This is the time for you to make calls asking specific questions to see how long it takes to return your calls or if you can reach them directly.

Only after all (3) of your FREE Bankruptcy Consultations will you decide which attorney is right for you.

If you don't really like any of them then it is time for your FREE Bankruptcy Consultation #4.

Essential #10: Filing of all previous years income tax returns prior to filing your Bankruptcy.

It is important to make certain that you have filed with the IRS for all years that have not been previously filed.

This must be done prior to filing your bankruptcy.

One thing that is not commonly known is the fact that IRS Debt can be discharged through your Chapter 7 Bankruptcy.

The rule that applies here is that you must have filed for all previous years prior to filing your Bankruptcy Petition.

The IRS Debt that can qualify for Discharge involves IRS debt that has been owed for at least (3) years prior to filing your Bankruptcy.

Also, be aware that the IRS Debt must be for Income taxes and not payroll related or specific other types of IRS Tax Debt.

You need to talk with your Bankruptcy Attorney for more information on this subject.

Frequently Asked Questions

QUESTION: When filing Chapter 7 or Chapter 13 Bankruptcy is it a good idea to keep very much surplus money deposited in my bank account or anywhere that is traceable?

ANSWER: No matter what chapter of bankruptcy you are filing do you really think it is a wise idea in the current hostile bank & creditor climate to show additional money anywhere? In Chapter 7 bankruptcy you are saying you have to file because you are insolvent and thus have no money!

In a Chapter 13 you are saying you only have enough money to afford the plan payment you are making - so where is this extra money in your bank account(s) coming from?

If you are filing Chapter 13 and have a business then of course you will need to have operational funds in your accounts. In a Chapter 13 this is different from Chapter 7 where you can only have only minimum funds available to you.

Remember you may need to substantiate any funds you have that are in excess of those amounts you have claimed on Schedules I and J.

ALWAYS DISCUSS ANY QUESTIONS WITH YOUR BANKRUPTCY ATTORNEY.

There are some cases where I have heard that many people convert any excess monies into American Express Travelers Checks or Cashiers Checks but it is probably preferable to keep the extra funds in a fire proof safe that is heavily secured.

QUESTION: Is it a good idea to transfer title to one of my cars over to my son before i actually file for bankruptcy next month?

ANSWER: if you transfer your car or other personal property of any real value just one month or even two months before you file your bankruptcy then what do you think this behavior will look like to the bankruptcy trustee?

If you don't want to give the bankruptcy court an impression that you are trying to commit fraud by changing ownership or title to property just prior to filing bankruptcy then I would avoid this kind of behavior.

There is a whole section on fraud and how to avoid it in "Ultimate Bankruptcy2010" that Discusses cases where others filing for bankruptcy have dealt with this issue and a whole lot more

QUESTION: How far in advance is an adequate amount of time to begin work on Pre-Planning my bankruptcy?

ANSWER: As soon as you know you might be filing for bankruptcy then "right now" is the best time to begin laying out your plans.

You will want to have the info available to decide first of all if bankruptcy is the best option you have for dealing with your financial situation.

If you conclude that YES filing for Chapter 7 or Chapter 13 Bankruptcy is your best solution then you would be wise to plan on about a SIX MONTH Pre Planning window.

If you think you cannot wait that long then PLEASE think again and ask yourself if you can really afford <u>not</u> to wait!

Before you begin making your plans please review my "Bankruptcy Control System" so that you are sure to control the Bankruptcy Filing Process from beginning to end.

You will find "Bankruptcy Control System" outlined in detail in "Ultimate Bankruptcy 2010" available in stores near you.

QUESTION: How can i postpone filing bankruptcy with so many creditors and collection agencies breathing down my neck?

ANSWER: Well, there are a number of ways you

can delay your filing but the one I recommend most involves your signing up with a local Consumer Credit Counseling Service (CCCS).

The number one reason for signing up with CCCS is that by doing so your behavior will more than likely be seen by the Bankruptcy Court as a legitimate attempt on your part to try and deal with your debt issues in a responsible manner.

In other words signing with CCCS will make you look good to the bankruptcy court and your creditors.

The second reason is that CCCS is also financed by the Credit Industry itself so they usually get their cooperation which means they can get these same eager creditors off of your back.

Also, you will have a good preparatory experience dealing with CCCS where you will have a good opportunity to sharpen your negotiation skills. CCCS will be working with you on what the amount of your plan payment will be with them so you will be required to supply them with income and expense figures.

You will need to negotiate expense figures you are willing to agree to in order to help determine the amount of your plan payment.

This is all part of the information you will use with your "Bankruptcy Control System" as outlined in Ultimate Bankruptcy 2010".

Remember; Practice Makes Perfect - Right?

QUESTION: Is one bankruptcy chapter less detrimental to my credit than another?

ANSWER: The answer to this question is kind of convoluted in that it seems just the opposite of what you might believe. If the level of your credit rating is a key area of importance to you when filing bankruptcy then Chapter 7 is definitely the chapter you want to file under!

Why? Well if you file a Chapter 13 bankruptcy you are going to be involved in a payment program that will last from (3) to (5) years!

What that means is that if you plan on repairing your credit score after filing bankruptcy ... you will not be able to re-establish your credit for about 5 ½ years from the date of filing ... NOT GOOD!

On the other hand if you file Chapter 7 Bankruptcy then you can begin repairing your credit just one month after Bankruptcy discharge or around 3 months at the most after initially starting your bankruptcy - process – THAT SOUNDS BETTER!

Why? Chapter 13 is a plan payment that lasts at least (3) years and today typically (5) years!

Chapter 7 Bankruptcy is a total discharge of all debt and is over once you have had your hearing and receive your discharge which occurs around one month after the hearing.

QUESTION: If i am in a Chapter 13 Bankruptcy where my Plan includes my auto lease payments and for whatever reason my case gets dismissed then what will happen to my car?

ANSWER: The real question you need to be asking is just how much more time will you have before the auto lease company sends a tow truck over to repossess your vehicle?

If you have a purchased vehicle with your auto loan payment in you Bankruptcy Plan then the car payments have more than likely only been partial for the entire term of the plan up to the date of the court dismissal!

In order to save your car you will very likely need to get an agreement with the auto finance or leasing company with the help of your bankruptcy attorney.

You will no doubt need to bring your lease current by paying the leasing company a one time payment. Remember to have all details agreed to in writing in advance and signed by an authorized representative of the lease company.

If you can get their assistance have your Bankruptcy Attorney assist you with this matter.

I do not recommend any form of direct discussion with the leasing company until you have in hand the entire amount of money that is currently past due!

Remember that we are in the electronic age and so if your lease is through one of the large leasing companies like Honda Credit or one of the other big boys you may only have a couple of days or less before repossession!

I know of one case where the attorney did not bother to call or e-mail their client to warn them of their case dismissal and before notice had arrived in the mail their car had already been towed away!

This happened in a matter of a single day so beware!

What happens if you want to keep your car and need more time in order to get your funding and stuff together?

Well I have heard of more than a few cases where potential victims of overly aggressive lease companies have simply stored their car in the garage of a friend until they were able to deal with the situation effectively.

What do i mean by effectively?

Until the person was able to borrow or save up enough money to bring their existing auto lease/loan current.

In this way they made certain not be left without transportation for work and as a result they were not forced to sacrifice their employment (means of survival) in any way.

QUESTION: Can I load my withholdings from my paycheck with exemption related items like optional profit-sharing deductions, maxed out 401K deductions, maxed out optional retirement funds, maxed out health benefits and any other options I can find to lower my take home income so that I can qualify for Chapter 7 bankruptcy over chapter 13?

ANSWER: Well sure, you can try just about anything you want to but please do not be surprised if the Bankruptcy Trustee forces you to remove all non-mandatory deductions!

If this happens and the Trustee does make such a requirement then just be aware you are exposed ... and it will be very difficult to come up with an explanation for adding other expenses or income losses once you have shown your hand in the bankruptcy process.

It is always better to pre-plan and work with an attorney so that this sort of thing never happens with your case. There is really no good reason to gamble with this matter because a Chapter 13 Bankruptcy (5) year payment plan can be very expensive and very hard on you and your entire family.

QUESTION: Can your IRS Debt be discharged through the Chapter 7 or Chapter 13 Bankruptcy Process?

ANSWER: YES ... but ... There are certain rules that apply but the main one for past due income tax is that the IRS Debt must have been owed at least 3 years prior to the filing of bankruptcy. Secondly, the debt must be income tax related and not related to payroll taxes or other non-standard taxes.

As with all key questions related to the bankruptcy process, please discuss this matter WITH YOUR BANKRUPTCY ATTORNEY!

Only a reputable Bankruptcy Attorney is qualified to answer this and all questions that are legal in nature.

QUESTION: Do I really need a "Bankruptcy Attorney" in order to get the kind of accurate information I need regarding bankruptcy law and procedure or for filing my bankruptcy case or will any practicing Attorney be ok?

ANSWER: If you are in need of a heart transplant would it be ok to use a general intern who is not a surgeon?

Law is filled with many specialized areas and disciplines and each one has its own set of special requirements. If you look in your yellow pages or on line you will see that most law offices specialize in key areas.

I feel that the best Bankruptcy Attorney is the one who works entirely in the bankruptcy arena and knows his practice and how the local trustee makes decisions based upon their interpretation of the bankruptcy law!

Personally I would never recommend going to a general practice law office unless that law firm has a special staff of attorneys who practice bankruptcy and nothing else and would have the experience and expertise to handle my case flawlessly.

If I were a heavy hitter and had a large amount of capital or assets and could afford it I would go to the law office where one of the trustee's actually practices and hire that trustee as my Bankruptcy Attorney.

Why?

No trustee is going to hassle another trustee because, in fact, they are all part of a social club that kind of watches each others back and is supportive in many ways.

Plus, who is going to know more about bankruptcy law and what is and is not acceptable more than one of the persons who over see's it all?

ALSO: Be certain that the attorney you end up retaining is available to you when you call on them!

Any attorney who does not return telephone calls in a timely manner or avoids talking with their clients is not the attorney who I want working for me!

Word of mouth may very well be your best form of referral.

Also, beware of "Attorney Referral Services" who are often set up by local Attorney's as a source for acquiring new client referrals!

If that is the case then you are only being referred to an attorney by a single attorney or group of attorneys who run the referral service in order to get new clients.

WORD OF MOUTH MAY BE YOUR VERY BEST BET IF YOU CAN GET IT.

Also, be sure you know why the people giving references like the Bankruptcy Attorney they are recommending.

An Attorney conducting Friendly discussions about their latest time on the golf course or "that 49'ers game" is not a good reason to retain an attorney.

MORE BONUS ITEMS

The following section contains (2) powerful Bankruptcy Tools you will definitely want to use when planning and preparing all key elements of your Bankruptcy!

PLEASE STUDY THEN EDIT THESE FORMS AS THEY RELATE TO YOUR OWN PERSONAL SITUATION THEN PRINT OUT FOR YOUR OWN PERSONAL USE.

General Bankruptcy Work List – PRINT

Total Number of Unsecured Creditors _____

Total Amount of Unsecured Debt $ _____
(credit cards, store charges, gas casino credit accounts, credit cards, etc)

Total Number of Secured Creditors _____

Total Amount of Secured Debt $ _____
(Including: home mortgages, auto loans & leases, boat loans, furniture store accounts, home electronics, major appliances, etc)

Number of Homes/Real Estate Owned _____

Primary Residence Value $ _____

Amount of Mortgage $ _____

All Other R.E. Values $ _____

All Other R.E. Loans $ _____

Total Number of Vehicles Owned _____

Amount of Auto Loan $ _____

Value All Other Autos $ _____

Total of All Auto Loans $ _____

Total Number of RV's owned _____

Including: Boats, Motorhomes, Mobile homes, Dirt Bikes, Motorcycles, Gliders, Jet Ski's, Dune Buggies, Snow Mobiles, etc

Total Value All RV's $ _____

Total Owed All RV's $ _____

Total IRS/Gov Debt $ _____

Non-Dischargeable Owed $ _____
(Including: Child Support, Spousal Support, School Loans, DUI Related Debt, etc)

Debt Created past 90 Days $_____
(See "Ultimate Bankruptcy 2010 on Recently Created Debt)

Total Unsecured Debt $ _____
(Credit Card, Store Charges, Doctor & Medical Bills, etc)

Total Secured Debt $ _____

Total Priority Debt $ _____
(Priority Debt is debt that generally cannot be discharged through bankruptcy and includes things like child support, spousal support, school loans, some IRS Debt, etc – see "Ultimate Bankruptcy 2010" for more detail on this matter)

Total Value of Contracts/Partnerships, etc $ _____

Total Combined Family Annual Income $ _____

Total Income from Rental Property or other $ _____

Critical Questions List - PRINT

This is a General List of Questions that need to be asked during your Free Bankruptcy Consultations with a qualified Bankruptcy Attorney.

Go through this list and only leave questions that are relevant to your own particular situation and remove those that are not. ADD any questions not found here that are relevant to your own particular needs. PRINT OUT THIS FORM AND USE DURING YOUR FREE CONSULTATIONS.

- What Chapter of Bankruptcy can I file with my current financial situation?

- How does the "Means Test" affect my bankruptcy filing? (see forms on page 69 of "Ultimate Bankruptcy 2010")

- Is the "State Median Income" amount based on gross income (before taxes & withholding) or net income (after taxes & withholding)?

- How will my "real income" be determined by the Bankruptcy Court?

- Can I keep (or surrender) my house?

- Will I have to pay any of my debts once I have filed?

- Will I have to pay my second mortgage on my home?

- What about my IRS debt?

- What about my School Loan Debt?

- Can I keep my Cars?

- What about my Car Payments?

- Can I keep my Retirement?

- Can I prevent IRS or other Wage Garnishments?

- Can I prevent Liens on my property?

- What if I have a lien on my property will It be removed?

- Can I keep my Personal Collections (coins, guns, antiques, jewelry)?

- Can I keep my Boat, RV, Trailer, etc?

- What Happens to payments on Boat, RV, Trailer, etc?

- Can I keep my tools that I use for my work?

- What about future money or property that I may receive in wills from family members?

- Can I keep my interest in my business partnership?

- What about property that belongs to a business/partnership I am involved with?

- What happens to child support payments I owe?

- What happens to spousal support payments I owe?

- What happens with hospital bills that I owe?

- What happens with medical bills that I owe?

- What happens If I want to pay a particular family doctor in order to keep their services for my child or other family member?\

- What happens to an ambulance bill I have with the county?

- What about debts I have with my dentist?

- Can I pay back money I owe to family members/friends prior to filing my bankruptcy?

- What happens to a car where the loan/title is listed in my name but all payments have been made by son/daughter/friend and the vehicle actually belongs to them? (I just took out the loan for them)

- Can I keep the Antique furniture that I own?

- Can I keep my life insurance plan?

- Can I keep my health insurance plan?

- What happens to my 401K and Retirement/Pension Accounts?

- What exactly is the "Means Test" and how will it affect my bankruptcy filing?

- How will my spouses Social Security Income affect my means test income and my bankruptcy in general?

- What happens to my accounts that have been turned over to collection agencies?

- How will the bankruptcy rules affect me and my wife since we are now living separately but still married?

- What happens if my spouse is filing for bankruptcy on debts that were owed prior to our marriage?

- What kind of income deductions will the bankruptcy trustee allow me to continue making that are related to my retirement/health insurance/profit sharing?

- Do I have to report "under the table" income that I have?

- ADD YOUR OWN QUESTIONS BELOW:

_____

_____

_____

_____

_____

_____

_____

_____

_____

www.ingramcontent.com/pod-product-compliance
Lightning Source LLC
Chambersburg PA
CBHW081226170526
45165CB00009B/2963